The Long Email To America

Where Are Your "Voices"

Kisha A. Brown

Can you see me, You kill my flesh and bones

just because I do not look like you, Can

You see me , Because of rote behavior and

what your daddy said you hate me , Can you

see me, Or is it much deeper you cannot be me,

so you hate yourself and your trying to kill the

you that , you cannot be, Can you see me , You

tried to steel our Town of Music , and even tried

to Trump our speeches. Can you See me, Our

innocence and freedom taken wrongly accused,

Can you see me , Now they are letting us out ,so

you decide to kill us instead. Racism never went

anywhere as one said, now it is just being

Tubed. Yeah, you can see me and your

scared,still hiding behind a sheet and a shield.

Can you see me

Where Are Your "Voices"

Are you stating to me that among all of you that

is in the industry and have a voice. Only a few

of you are stepping up to the plate. You have

fear that your Chews will be taken away and

there will be no more Fridays that are pink. Or

you that was once Iced now is to sweet like

southern Tea to speak. Where are you now ,all

of you that kept silent. Not the minister that is

related Benjamin small but packs a big punch he

risked being ostracized but he was always a

Revolutionary soul, while all you so called hard

core people sleep. You even got the beautiful

people risking contracts and concerts, Her

mother is from Alabama , Her father is from

Louisiana , something like that and you Whaps

of Confetti and Waynes of little have no words.

Until it is your city, I suppose, We should be

peaceful like my not so Uncommon brother and

the Legend. They just keep killing us ,but only

when there is retaliation on the cops then

something must be done. We were innocent , we

did nothing wrong , we are just of color and you decide we are not worth being on this planet so you kill us. And eye for and eye ,oh wait that only applies to olden times right. Much like the days of old people do not want change . they still can not believe that there is a man of color in office.

"You People" never wanted us to make it but still we rise like an Win-free, like the Smiths with a Jade, like our own black entertainment. Yes we believe that all lives matter. Why is it offensive to us for you to say that though, Can you come up with your own sh*t. Stop stealing from us ,again can I say the speech they tried to Trump. That other Hillary that is not swanked just is threatened by a strong smart women. Really even after the truth came out they continued to lie. "You People " said that it was

Gods will that we were slaves , as you told the

Indians convert or die. You want us to die so

you found a legal way to kill us. Then you

found a few house slaves that you brain washed

to help, so it does not look like just white cops

are killing us. Now I have friends of all different

races, often ask them if they came through town

saying lets round them up and kill them, would

they stand with they all say yes. However when

it comes to the police we stand on separate

sides, just listen and do what they tell you. Is

this before or after they shoot me.

"You People" when you are with your K family

your yelling racial slurs , and perpetuating hate.

When you see me by myself you try to sleep

with me. Are they mostly killing black men yes

,from the beginning of time. Do they kill black

women yes. This is the thing if you break the

back bone ,the body can not stand. That is the

way they want us. Not all white people are bad

and vice ,versa. For the cowards that hide

behind their sheets and badges. This is what has

been happening for years to you telling the

young children that , they can not make it do not

strive to be bigger that what you already are .

We have believed that lie for to long. We are

marching in the streets , ok while they teach

their children to shoot, and how to own legal

fire arms. They teach their children the stock

market , while we teach our children how to

work in the market. They teach their children

the importance of maintaining a good credit

score. We never knew we had one until we tried

to get a house or a car. There has been such a

brain washing in the world ,that we cannot see

the forest for the trees.

If we do not wake up it all will be lost ,our lives

, our children, our culture. These racist people

have children and grandchildren. In order for the

devil to get you, he cannot come with horns and

look horrible. No he has to come like the Trojan

Horse bearing gifts as we let our guard down as

they come to kill us. Trojan horse, police,

judge,lawyer,doctor,welfare,abortion

clinics,schools. All of them have a certain

percentage of corruption. I forgot to mention a

Giant Trojan Horse religion. Yes all have their

level of corruption nothing or no entity is

infallible. I have yet to see some of you stand up

,you have family and friends that can benefit

from you just saying stop the madness. These

poor people that are dying , when they saw your

films you said thank you, when we listened and

bought your music you again say thank you. I

saw you helping in Louisiana to build houses

how wonderful, was a just a tax right off or just

another way for you to make sure you don't fall

in B Pitt.

I saw you step up ,many of you in the Orlando

tradgedy you raised two million in a few days

for the families. More than a hundred unarmed

black people have been killed since 2015 by

police. It is only July and the police have killed

a hundred and thirty six black people in 2016.

However let me be fair , over two hundred white

males have been killed in the last two years by

police officers. The same reason they killed

them back then , because they refuse to be

racist. Our very existence is being threatned and

our lives ruined by these tragedies. Long has

gone the The King, The Ali, The Marvin,The X,

unfortunate demise of the beautiful not so

Bland. We must unite and stand together ,

marching is ok but it is not as effective as it

once was. So that has brought me to this not so

lighted place. Where are your voices I hear

nothing from you we hear nothing from you.

What will it take for you to finally step up and

talk, no you have no obligation but when your

sons and daughters die for the same reasons,

don't expect a letter of grief and sorry. You lay

dormant while the one that use to be a Master

has his Romeo driving the bullet want care who

he is related to. Remember while you are a top

Dogg your sons are still endangered species.

Even though you are in your own Village of

Nellie you have sons to. The I.T. guy you have

sons and daughters.

You have to understand that although some of you may be famous to us,some people don't know you, they definitely don't know your children. Yes it sounds like I am angry and I am , I am tired of feeling like I am in season. Every time I hear the new now or read it , did they kill another one of us today. Yes us ,even if I don't know you personally ,my heart still loves you and cries for you when I see you have suffered tragedies and loss all over the world. I lived up North for my entire young life and then I move to Florida,whoa it is not the tourist attraction state all the time . They are so behind time racially , that I can see my great , great, grandmother. I can hear her saying don't let them kill you. Or is that Mad Dea with her gun telling me to turn around and shoot I don't know. I don't know if I will ever understand as of yet what it means to be rich , but when I am I surely hope that I use whatever platform given to me . I would want to speak out on injustices I believe in.

We go about our daily lives as if , when the

smoke clears the injustices have faded away.

We see police officers trying to humanize

themselves, posing for pictures with their

children. Nice little set up right , let your guard

down right. You better not , they are still there

finding any reason they can to take away your

rights,your dignity and your freedom. It has

only been a short time since we have been given

our rights. It has not even been a hundred years

yet , don't confuse what the Abe put on paper as

true freedom ,because it wasn't. It is when the

Luther stepped up and demanded equality and

not just freedom ,changes started to come. We

keep trying to be eagles but you cannot soar

with a rock on your back. You hate to say those

things like it will never change , well I am

hoping one day it will. However it would have

be a great thing like the ,dinosaurs dying in

order for that to happen.

Every racial inequality on the books that was once law that they never took off, making it illegal to marry outside of your race, after dark you have to stay on this side of the tracks "Sea Bring" the bell will sound when it is time. I could not even go to a friends wedding because the family was prejudice,but she is going to have children and of course you would hope the children will grow up in a wonderful environment , one filled with love of others and tolerant of differences. See it is not enough to just be in loving home , because they seem to

love each other but not others of difference.

These same people that are prejudice again

don't just work for the police department, they

work for Children and Family Services, court

systems and so on and so on. In order to keep a

society down they must not just infiltrate the

system but control it. Now I vote , but does it

really count we have what is called the U.S.

Electoral College in order to win you need a

majority of 270 electoral votes and they decide

the vote. I know what they do but I don't know

who they are.

Now your city and mine have votes on things

all the time , when do they hold these votes

mostly when hard working people are going to

work or too tired to attend. So when you see those signs up about a meeting try to go. When you pass by what use to be a playground and now it is a bowling alley, now they have kicked you out of the process and once its done it is done. People you never met ,whom will never even give you the time a day decide where your children go to school, where you are going to live and how and what kind of transportation will be provided. I am convinced the more you know , the more you hate and the more cynical you become. You can try to become more active

and give your community and you a voice. It is

not just the lack of knowledge it is the lack of

involvement, the it is not my problem mentality

has cost us so much. I can trust them instead of

checking and researching who they really are

and what they stand for.

The Wall of Mart a stolen dream,Donald of

Mac,Chicken of Kentucky,the Kings of Bugers

all stolen dreams. How long is going to be , that

we keep silent how much more is it going to

take. Terrorist are recruiting our citizens

because it looks better on the bad side. We don't

stand together so why should anyone else listen

to us. They see themselves as a family, no

matter what each other look like they share a

common goal. The first thing you ever hear out

of some ones mouth that is from another country

, why should I listen to an American they don't

even like each other. We have lost our voice

,our footing our what it means to be a member

of the human race. Cyber bullying ,text message

or social media period a faster way to get hate

out there and to recruit more people that can

learn to hate with you. Now if you were a Kim ,

that had a driven mother and was able to steer

the hate towards success for you so be it. Love

and Hate are very powerful emotions but

combining them makes for wars and killing

across the United States. We are so much not

what we have been calling ourselves were

becoming the Divided States because we have

to separate everything we come in contact with

Democrats , Republicans. Why cant it be we are

running for the people and who ever wins is the

best canidate , running with one common goal.

That's right that's laughable ,but we are suppose

to be United. You cannot stand if your back is

broke. Social Media has joined us ,but it is good

and bad that comes with that with a click,of a

like or dislike you can change the outcome of

someone's day.

"You People " in Washington that are making

all of these decisions and got all the money. Do

you even go to the places where your making all

of these decisions ,where you are making a

decision on what to do or what not to do,yes I

know we have representatives but sometimes

you must not listen to them. I feel like a snail in

Florida trying to go up the highway. Your

solution is no welfare , well are you going to

educate and give jobs to those who are not on

welfare anymore. Yes they may have had to

many children ,yes their life is of their own doing. A whole bunch of people and there children not on welfare anymore , sounds good , until you start having to provide for the high crime rate and desperate people are angry people ,waiting for you and your family to come out of the house and take what they cant make. Your solution has a flaw. Provide a transitional solution ,a job to pay for your bills and possible training to get you through that transition.

We are not your children , you make decisions

then you leave us out of them ,not an email or

thirty day notice even. I did not do this but if I

did want to do something to counter act all this

killing ,which I did not , I'm coming for you,

coming for you , heres my gun ,heres my gun.

Zimmer not a man, is free , not so Merry land ,not guilty. I am tired of hearing about you on a plane getting kicked off the plane for using a box Christopher,you use to Wow me with your little rhymes now you cant vote because your mixed, tired of that , what you ate a restaurant at Democratic convention,how you hate each other. Hip Hop of some kind of love on display as wild crazy sex addicts that guess what hate each other surprise. I keep listening to see who is going to stand up and hear their voice I am waiting. So far My daddy Louisiana My mother

Alabama gets kudos in the streets all over the

United states of America. Thank you for

speaking for us !

You ,that use to be Sharp now your dull , you go

where ever the paper takes you. You, one of the

Jacksons looks like you will say yes to anything

that gives you the right amount. We are

becoming a land of use to be s' and I use to talk

but now I'm afraid, I will lose my money and

my "Those People" as friends.

Even the beautiful Berrie has been misquoted as saying, she will never procreate with a darker skinned man In order to give her children a chance in society, they have to be light white in order to have money to fight. If said , do not be surprised she is not the first to make this decree. It is a still a dimwitted notion. They name you something cute like malato ,half breed, and one fourth. It does not matter how ever fair , to the ones that is prejudice and hate it is not up for

debate.

When they see pale or dark it is a bounty on

your head and oh yes they still want you dead.

Even the Carrie has faded in the untouchable

category she thinks , because of all that money

she has allowed herself to be clouded. Your

children will have to still grow up if fortunate

enough to,and they will want to drive but

because they are half Can-non they will stop

them and ask aren't you too young to have all of

this cash. Bullets are plenty to go around and

they have you in sight , for their next round.

Still you remain silent because they would have

you think ,they accept you as long as you don't

look like your two.

You want an unreality show become black or a

mixed couple for a day. Without your

entourage, drive in an upscale neighborhood or

a not so nice neighborhood. Would you be afraid? I think yes because your reality is not mine, if you step out of your comfort that confines. It seems to be worst because it is in the south ,but the hate even migrates.   Even if it is legal ,but hidden open and illegal killing from Africa to Syria the system is set up to kill in the same way. Kill those who are different and those that oppose.

The eradication of out race started long ago, it started first to take our identity and our spirits. To believe that we are nothing and will never be anything. However "You People" are mad at that man we all know as Commander and Chief and the one to be because in your twisted head she is just another lover of the Brother.

Yes I know I am already a target because of what I look like , why make trouble. I have to use the only thing I have and it is "My Voice." I have to try to do a reprogramming of sorts, my youth to have caution of the police. Not to give trust or respect if it is not earned.

I know some of the most beautiful, handsome people of color are in charge of the police departments in various states. They say listen and you will not get hurt. They have no reason to shoot or pull their weapons , if you do exactly what they tell you. Now what do you say we listened and they killed us anyway. I am

listening "Where are Your Voices".

"You People" you say you are coming to help

us, but you divide and separate us. Nothing new

to you , this has always been your purpose and

plan. Still you think we ae not human, in secret

you still away our children, to use for your own

personal slaves, so what their seven or eight .

You are okay with that injustice until you get

caught. You scream it is a better life then what

they have seen. So you say , but that is the life

you chose for them. I warn you those that have

not been caught in the trafficking of these

beautiful people. A day is coming when they

will rise up and had enough. They will turn

against you with the knives of the food that you

use to cut. You try to beat the life out of them ,

their hopes their dreams. So they dream another

and it involves the killing of you and to help

each other. Who can be told , because as far as

anyone is concerned a person that does not exist

cannot kill. When you hear and read this know

that everything they told you is a lie. Get Out!

"You People" we keep your attention when we

are in entertainment or sports. Even though our

position and status earned our cars and houses.

Your once love for us turns again to what you

know and that is hate , jealousy and contempt.

Like it is your money we have spent. So you

start a campaign to discredit us and take away

what we have made. The fall of giants with set

ups and lies. The unfortunate thing is they don't

see it until it is too late.

Until the Tiger was in the Woods, or until

Jorden river was parted,until the Coby was

tanted,the Sapp poured out of the trees,the sugar

Browns and the Gas of old, the one that Parked

the Eve of his Lagoriah. The other Barryer that

might have been between them,The Gibson that

had the Keys of the City of Cole.in his hands,

the George that crossed that was never a

Washington that crossed the Rivers, the Wade in

the water that almost missed his Union, the

Odometer that stopped for the Car-Dash-Ean,

even the King of James does not recognize the

heat, the Great Shack even fell blaming

someone else for the ringing of the bell. They

don't see it the attempt of and sometimes their

success to separate the family.

The plan of eradication starts with family and

our fathers being taken away. Without the

backbone, the body cannot stand. We women

are strong don't get me wrong, but " We are

Stronger together."

The music tried to warn us years ago The SrK
One, how they found a legal way to enslave,
how there was no difference between overseer
and officer they are one in the same. They make
the message fade away with the music of today,
as " You People" influence the media and the
news and have the controlling interest , you can
still walk down an Aile as long as no one
questions your authority, you can still be top
dog.

Did you influence the now messages of hoes,

cars and money. A far cry are the messages of

togetherness and hope. Messages of disgrace

and egocentric development linger because of

the fear of not having a payday oh how we have

sold out and strayed. The it is not my problem

mentality: I am getting a check f*ck a role

model,keep buying my music and tickets that is

all I care about. " Where ae Your Voices".

Silenced like sheep bringing brought to

slaughter. The Make –a – Beth stands up at the

Democratic Convention another beautiful

women of color. Like my ma from Alabama my

daddy Louisiana.

The Can –I – go – Wests speaks on Jesus

walking and the injustices of that he thought

was Swift. I don't hear you now. Do have to

scream ? I got the dollars then , you will say

something. Or does it have to take for your

compass to be killed or hung because of her

beautiful complexion. Then you will come to us

and want us to pray with you and we will. Even

though you have abandoned us Can-I –go –

West.

Just like anything else a campaign is given, for

hate , for bullying and to cause mass

destruction, These are all learned behaviors ,

and there are hard choices to be made. One way

or another whether it is our beliefs or our

choices we as people have strong convictions .

We expect everyone else to follow suit with our

beliefs. This is the way it has always been, if it

is not broke do not fix it. Do not make waves,

mind your own business and stay out of it.

This attitude has kept us enslaved and kept us without protection. It seems as though it is open season on people of color and the ones that stand with them. It has to be a great change that takes place in our society. We say we are free ,but we are entangled in our own web of pain and insecurity ,that is what causes others to hate with no reasoning.

"Where are Your Voices"

We know we can make it in this world. We need

education or the willingness to learn a skill to

be a productive member of society. I know

what you want, I hear it all the time go back

where you came from. You want us to kill each

other off one way or another. You give us drugs

and then put us in jail for selling them. Yes it is

wrong but if his story teaches us anything. We

did not bring the drugs here or ourselves. Now

you want us dead , because of what you feared

all along , once freed in our minds and our

behaviors we can achieve more than you could ever believe. Except for William who is the Mayor he seems to believe in us and I like his style.

"You People " try to divide us with your lies and the creation of your stereotypes. You keep trying to break us with your days of old tactics. I too almost was a victim of reacting to your hate. Until a man I "Esteemed as Joel" started pouring into me sounds of victor and not a

victim. I didn't want to listen at first because I

lumped him into "You People" . My hate was

growing strong to the point of being unaffected

of the tragedies of officers losing their lives for

no reason. I am not going to lie , I wanted them

all to die even the good ones were guilty by

association. Yes it is illogical, but no more

illogical than someone killing us because of

their fear or my color. For them obeying the law

as they were taught and they are still dead. It

hurt every time I saw a cop car, I wanted to stop

slow down and just shoot.

I was preparing myself mentally for prison , I

spent time with my family so they could be

remember as the good person as I once was.

This is of course the kind of reaction "You

People" want. I decided to take a more

constructive route and I will speak all of the

country. I will try to be the next voice. My

family too cannot survive in a proper manner "

without the backbone the body will not

function". I just could not just keep doing

nothing , while they killed children. Everyone I

looked at my children, my brother , my family

they all could be next. Did I stop believing in

God? No , I just stop listening. Of course I did

not kill anyone. "?" I met some great police

officers by design , while on my way to do the

damage I thought was do to all , that vowed to

protect and serve. North Carolina had a

beautiful lady officer that wept at the tragedy,

but is caught in the middle between loyalty and

duty. From New York, Maryland and

Washington. They fall between both sides of the

argument. When not in uniform are stopped by

other officers and while in the police station are

still ,discriminated against.

They cannot go on record saying anything, the

police situation seems to be dealt with in the

departments. Of course this is not a new

problem, but there has been no solution. They

are under paid and over worked. So was I , do

something else then. Stop making excuses for

incompetence, mediocrity, prejudice and down

right stupidity.

Trying to uphold the law and speak out

expressing your first amendment rights,gets you

fired and reprimanded. If you break the back

bone the body cannot stand. You can run for

President and insult everyone, and be the

biggest jerk on earth. Your own party dislikes

you,when you utter the words African American , my flesh crawls. Na-ke-yah Jonesenburg got fired for speaking out abot racial equality and speaking against the divide that exist within the police department. Again I can run for president and it is okay to be Trumped.

How can you remain silent ,it is a catastrophic thing that is taking place in this America. You say if you come here you can follow your dreams. This is only true if it does not interfere with your own. Only if you get to stand on our

backs and parade us around like the show dogs ,

"You People" believe we are. No More!!!! We

are taking back our America. We are

strong,united and educated and we see you.

Your weakened by your own failed attempts to

ensure we become exactly what you believe us

to be.

Mon-key see Mon-key do , yes,the Mon-key is

you.

Unless we change our mentality as a nation as a

people. It is just a perpetuating , revolving door

of hate and fear. Fear if we do not conform,to

what " You People" want. Like straight hair and

fair skin acceptable in some sectors another

failed attempt to separate us. The dark skinned

beautiful woman that changes her

appearance,because she believed the lie of she is

not good enough,or she was not chosen as the

one to be with.

Oh "Kym" not so little,you were always

beautiful. To the mothers who do not

know,what to call their children that are biracial.

In this world they would have you always

questioning your identity. Your what your father

is as they say in the south, as if your mother

does not exist. They tell you that your

complexion determines your race. Even if you

come from the same father and mother. We are

different shades of color, but we refuse to keep

being labeled by the colors you give us. Like

"The black beautiful bird" that started as a

"Cos-bey. They give us these titles every three

to ten years.

" You People" called us not human,then three fouths,ni**er,negro,black,Afro American and now African American. Just titles not set in truth,they also use to call Irish people that use to have dark hair and dark complexion black Irish. I was not born in Africa and some are offended, because it is not a distinction. You can be born of pale skin and have migrated from Africa and now African American , like a pastor name "Rod-knee" Brown and wife Anika Brown. I don't want to be defined by what you say I am , because of your flawed thinking. Until I am

able to retrace my whole family tree, I am

Indian, Haitian, Jersey American.

Separation should not be our common goal ,the

last time I checked we are human first. We see

but we are blinded by our own insecurities

"Where are your voices". Other people threaten

to kill US not just a certain kind of US.

Being unified should be our common goal,but

ignorance and fear has always been on the plate

of destruction. For whatever reason "You

People" will never let us be it seems. You

continue to separate us economically,socially

and racially within our own race and have done

it successfully and effortlessly for so long now

you wish we continue to rotely follow. No

more! My ancestors may have died but they

have imprinted on me , to fight for what is right.

Why live in fear,if you die for what you believe

in , then you have done what is right. Why "You

People" say because I too have a dream.

For me to get all the knowledge I can and they

cannot X it out of me because I am passing it

on. That I am not confound by your restrictions

because of what I look like. Thank you again the

man I "Esteem as Joel". Never forget who you

are learn the past so you don't repeat it . Mark-

us-Oh Great Gar-vee. No greater agony than

bearing inside of me an untold story. My-Angel-

of –ooh.

This may not be a big book ,but it is what needs to be said,or would "You People". Rather I be silent instead. I know you would rather I be dead. I have a different view,all of you are not bad. Please forgive me my eye view is tainted and cynical too. I am trying to get a better look at you.

Some people say it is better to be with your own kind,rewind the rainbow shows us love comes in all kinds. For a minute I thought we were all human,my mistake I forget the plate of what they eat is hate.

I watch the news and my mind goes in reverse. Another brother or sister gone in a hearse. Don't know how much more I can take, because it is contagious this thing called hate. I do not wish to become as the people that keep their soul in unrest,because I promised my ancestors I would

do my best.

WHERE ARE YOUR VOICES: People we look up to , So afraid of losing their soles, and their golds. Again long is gone my lyricist of old. Don't make the mistake that I am prejudice a touch, that would be,a bit too much. Am I one sided though,only time will tell and only you will know.

"You People" Stop killing us ,Because as some of us will march,"Others" However may get that Spark.

Please don't make that mistake because even

"You People" have hearts.

The Forward : Why I wrote this book it is quite simple , if no one steps up everyone suffers. You cannot keep waiting for someone else to invoke change, we have to be the conversation starter sometimes. Just because it is a hard subject or it may be uncomfortable and may even spark some anger . It is relevant and necessary. We need more leaders, everyone is stuck in their own little bubble not wanting it to pop. United we Stand divided without a backbone We fall.

Dedicated : To all of the Fallen Soldiers , that lost their lives to Fear and Prejudice. Remember respect is not given ,it is earned on both sides. Who matters? We all matter.

Description of Book : I entitled it Where Are

Your Voices. As I looked at the media and the

different personalities that exist in it. I failed to

see or hear anyone standing up. Except for a

very few ,in order to invoke change we have to

stand as a majority. So I named,but not named

some people that I thought failed to stand up.

The ones I believe as cowards , that only stand

for something if it puts them in the lime light. I

got tired of hearing about another black person

killed and how some people are starting to see

as a reality and taking it so lightly. Whether it is

a black and white thing or just a blue thing.

Something needs to change. As I began this

journey in anger it still remains , but my

platform on which I decided to take has

changed.

About the Author: I am a mom , a sister and a grandma. The only thing I can imagine is every time the phone rang I would get one of those phone calls those poor mothers got. I have worked hard since I was eleven. I have voted since I was old enough too. I have been in social media in the shadows with no real impact. Hoping that someone would stand up. Knowing that it may be backlash is ok. If I continue to remain comfortable and silent my voice will die with me. Just arguments among piers and social media not. I want to make a difference a change,

I do not care to continue to say , it is just the

way things have been and this is the way it is

going to stay. I will not be one of those people

that cry on the sidelines and look to someone

else for the change , it did not start with me and

I am praying it does not end with me.

Kisha Brown